Progressive Lines Etched in Time's Brittle Glass

A Collection of Injustice Poetry

Shelby "Mahogany" Wilson

Edutainment
Nite
Publishing

Progressive Lines Etched in Time's Brittle Glass

Published by Edutainment Nite Publishing in 2026

Copyright © 2026 by Shelby "Mahogany" Wilson

Book Cover by Reginald G Wilson

Edutainment Nite Publishing

First Edition 2026

ISBN: 979-8-9903692-8-3

❀ Formatted with Vellum

Dedication

I would like to honor the people who raise awareness in our community. Those creating spaces to celebrate and uplift people of color. I recognize pioneers like Betty Davis and Marquita Pierre McAlister. I send a special thanks to Shirley Mae Staten. She continues to honor her crafts in music and art. Opening doors for youth and the disadvantaged.

I honor the women actively working in this community to provide service and education one event at a time. Jasmin Smith has moved tirelessly to highlight the issues while earning a seat at the table. She organizes events to teach about generational wealth and provides spaces for people of color to share and support each other. I give special thanks to MoHagani Magnetek, a grassroots activist. She has set Alaska ablaze. She is constantly evolving and leaving new trails everywhere she goes. She continues to open doors for the LGBTQI+ community by providing opportunities to celebrate and showcase our talent.

I am honored to know or work with all these amazing people. Each has demonstrated that the power of action can spark change. I am inspired to keep the fire going through my words.

Contents

Voting Voice

Foreword

Shelby Wilson is a pillar within the literary and cultural community. For more than 20 years, she has dedicated her life to art, activism, and service, using her voice to create space for truth, healing, and connection. A dynamic performance poet and longtime Vice President of Black Feather Poets, Shelby's work is grounded in purpose and sustained by an unwavering commitment to community.

Her poetry is fearless and honest, shaped by lived experience and a deep understanding of responsibility. Shelby does not write to impress. She writes to bear witness, to challenge silence, and to remind others of their power. Her presence in the literary world has uplifted countless voices, particularly those often pushed to the margins.

This book reflects the same spirit that has guided Shelby's journey for decades. It is bold, intentional, and rooted in love for community. Through these pages, Shelby Wilson invites readers into a space of reflection, resilience, and unapologetic truth.

-- Jimmie Ware

Foreword

Poet • Mentor • Facilitator • Inspirational Speaker • Author

Queen's Pride

Queen's Pride

She Roars

It began decades ago on factory floors
Around the kitchen tables
Office lunch rooms
There were whispers, a humming
Slowing rumbling and now it's a roar
It's time
To purge the laws over our body
It's time
For equal pay for equal work
It's time to eliminate sexual harassment
without repercussion
Enough with the antiquated notion
Some jobs are only for men

The era has begun
Me too isn't just a response
It's a movement
Time's up is more than statement
It's a notification that change is on the horizon

Hashtag me too

Shelby "Mahogany" Wilson

Hashtag time's up
Hashtag enough
Hashtag she roars

The journey began a long time ago
Today it's ignited
Burning through the fog of uncertainty
We'll stand up against oppression
Rise up and confront misogyny
We will be heard
Not dismissed or ignored
It's time we are seen for our contributions
Respected for our opinions
Given a seat at the head of the table
From judges to governors
senators to representatives
We will replace State and Federal laws
The ones that prohibit our advancement

We are empowered
We are doers
We will infiltrate and create effective change
We are the United States of America
Not just America
Our patriotism runs deep in our soil
We have received the call to action
Hear her roar

It started decades ago with
Recy Taylor and Elizabeth Cady Stanton
Forging ahead with Crystal Lee Sutton
Opening doors for
Angela Davis and Tarana Burke
They paved the foundations with determination
Battling discrimination and retaliation

Progressive Lines Etched in Time's Brittle Glass

Yet she roars
re-designing this nation
Chipping away at cracks around the edges

Here we stand
For our sisters, our nieces
For all the women
Who will walk and talk after us
We will shatter
The glass ceiling in their name
Not with a scream
but with permanent change.
HEAR US ROAR.

Black Girl Magic

Bold and daring
Fierce and unapologetic
Magnificent presence
Ambition sprinkled with ingenuity
Classy with a touch of sassy
That's Black Girl Magic

Beauty is always underestimated
Unfiltered splendor
Curvaceous no matter what shape
Natural or weave
We slay it with ease
Light to dark melanin
Our skin is glowing
Personification of sophistication
Exquisite representation of God's creation
Black Girl Magic in formation

Passionate communicator
Driven to succeed
Vibrant personalities

Black Girl Magic

Professional finesse
Built in assertiveness
Walking with authority
Sauntering in grace
Black Girl power on display

Black Girl Magic

Facial expressions are serious
We invented Resting Bitch Face
Intense Mama glare
You better not stare
We are always on alert
Snap back game on point
Rolling of the neck perfected
Black Girl Magic in effect

Multitude of personalities
Different degrees of fabulosity
Greatness bundled in each body
Confidence shining brightly
Dominating queen on scene
The foundation and the glue
Inspiration in any situation
It's Black Girl Magic potion

We have been given seeds of greatness
Power of influence
Will to persevere
Motivation fueled by ancestors
Determination to prevail
We are a powerful manifestation
Beautiful fabrications never replicate
It's our individuality that stands us apart
Women with a hidden gift
Perfection wrapped in elegance
That's Black Girl Magic

Soul of the Community

Black women have always been
the backbone of the community
The foundational center of our culture
We wear our strength on our shoulders
Our voices tell the stories of our history
Threading the soul of the community
like a piece of quilt
Our very existence is deemed threatening
We are zealous and ambitious
Our power is intimidating
We are bold women with intention
Our voices are bombastic
We speak our mind
Our poise commands authority
We can be domineering
Our personalities are magnetic
We ooze charisma
We are wisdom speakers
Truth teachers
Tempered and measured
We are a dynasty of queens

Soul of the Community

Regal and refined
Sometimes it's a struggle to shine
Forging onward in silence
Raised to be resilient
Enduring physical and mental pain
Praying over our men as they are slain
Putting the shattered pieces back in place
Repurposing scrapes
Turning them into better situations
We have always been resourceful
We are the face of strength
Maternal protectors
inherited through bloodlines
Always on the verge
Cradling a fragmented community
Striving to maintain sovereignty
We are the pillars grounded in reality
Symbols of stability and reliability
Our very presence evokes vitality
We foster camaraderie
We are the cornerstone of the community
The leaders in the shadows
Wilding incredible power
We are the heart of the culture
Fragile yet essential
Our life rejuvenates and replenishes
We are more than the backbone
We are the soul of the black community

Black Is Not a Color

Black is the color of my hair not my skin
Texture of wool
Sometimes itchy and irritating
Like the negative thoughts borne about race
Black is absent of light
Yet when I enter the room
My smile is luminous
My presence brings warmth
My color is magnetic
I am the beginning of the rainbow
Radiant like the sun

Black is the color of my hair not my skin
Colored and perm
Weakening the dexterity of the hair
I'm good and pure to the heart
Black is depicted
Described in a derogatory nature among peers
To the corporate world
I am color, then woman, then person
I'm absent from definition

Black Is Not a Color

Negro, Black, African American
Are the titles used to describe me
Words no longer define
the multi-shade of people
Our ancestors reside on all continents
not just Africa
where the pigment darkens
from the sun's rays
Leaving bronze yellow and variations of tan

Black is the color of my hair not my skin
Coiled and nappy at the roots
Straightened to blend myself
into the Caucasian workforce
Only to resend when tested
To appear more docile in appearance
Innocence yet naïve
the games and secret communities
Which divides my brothers and sisters
Pitting us against one another
Teaching them to use their shoe
to smash their confidence
Destroying hope
Silencing all objections
Smothering opinions
One person can poison
A group conspiring can change history

Black is the color of my hair not my skin
Trained and conditioned
yet the roots remain resistant
What is talking "Black" or acting "Black"
Deprived of education tools and resources
Little children slipping through the cracks
Corrupting the vision through false idols

Black Is Not a Color

Stimulate the precious gems
by showing them by example
Encourage them through knowledge
It is America's hidden diamonds among the youth

Black is the color of my hair not my skin
Brittle from the harsh chemicals and water
My hair neither defines me
nor shapes my character
I'm absent from labels
Defined within the contours of my actions
Drawn out and clarified by
luscious lips filled with liquid
words to heal or hurt
My talent lies between them
Saturated with wisdom
Framed in a status face
Span of my nose and love in my eyes
Beautiful lively attractive creative being before you
Black is the color of my hair
but not my being
I'm a multicolored person
In a black and white world

Healing Strength

Today I called upon my ancestors
Give me strength
Give me power to smile
in the faces of my oppressors
People would rather have a white man lead
Instead of people like me
Reminding me
We are still less in the eyes of this country
The country that enslaved my ancestors
Stealing our people under false pretenses

Give me the words to speak
with love and kindness
Instead of the bitter hate that fills my bones
I call on the ancestors'
Our mothers and fathers
Those who had the will to make the journey
Those who fought and continued to fight

I stand with them hand in hand
Back-to-back

Healing Strength

Holding steady
Our cities are going unheard
Words float aimlessly falling on deaf ears
Lost among the money and influencers
Using churches and phony prophets to manipulate
Harboring feelings of persecution
Unworthiness

Healing Strength

Our value is being diminished but not tarnished
We have fallen many times only to rise taller
I call upon the spirits
Step with me into the world
Guide me through turmoil
Weighing in the waters of tears
I grieve the loss
I grieve for the misled

I ask those who stood on the path before me
Give me fuel to drive my ambition
Give me the will and wisdom
Guide me as I travel on this journey
through the flurry of bad information
False idolization
Give me the power to seek
something greater than temporary gratification

False sense of security
Bound me to a paycheck and inadequate health care
I seek the energy of all those who traveled before
To protect my sanity
Give me sight to see clearly
Lift me up so I too may stand with dignity
Breaking free
Give me power to be present in this broken society
This fight is greater than overcoming adversity
It's about healing humanity

Forgotten Pride

Huey Newton and Marcus Garvey got it right
Stand tall under the light
Our blackness is beautiful
Our contributions are endless
Yet our lives are deemed useless
We fought to gain every privilege
So, when our brothers and sisters are murdered
How do we expect the law to protect us
Constant stereotyping and dehumanizing
keeps us compartmentalized

Invisible chains
Our ancestors have ropes around our necks
Still believing in persistence
Education will merit acceptance
But our color never changes
They will degrade us behind our backs
If we are compliant
Our role in house will be reserved
Black Lives Matter
We keep asking for change

Forgotten Pride

What are we willing to sacrifice
What's the plan of action

Marcus and Huey had it right
We must stand up as a community
Hold the torch high
Rise up like Fred Hammon
Build foundations not institutions
Harriet Tubman showed us resilience
Fredick Douglas showed us knowledge is power
Thurgood Marshall created law
Martin and Malcolm taught us perseverance
Our ancestors are holding the light

Marcus and Huey had it right
Teach our youth our history 365 days a year
Show them we are a rainbow of diversity
From coiled hair to fair complexion
Our hands shaped this nation
Contributing to the American evolution
We do more than populate
We are producers, inventors, and creators
We are generations of transformation
Leaders of tomorrow
Our power is not a single application
It is the unification of the color nation
Our Ancestors show us fortitude
Compound with determination

Marcus and Huey had it right
Remember we were kings and queens
Before we were slaves
Descendants of greatness
Powerful representation
Call upon your ancestors

Forgotten Pride

Learn your history
Reclaim your glory
Stand tall
Be regal in the face of adversity
We are heirs of a noble tribe
It's time to embrace your African pride

Social Question

Unheard Voices

Their sounds vibrate in unison
escaping from cracks
Vocal cords wrapped by social bondage
Piercing the ears of those willing to hear
Listening to the details inflicted
As their voices peek through
Pounding at the doors of the lawmakers
Community advocates begging for recognition
Acknowledgment in a world
Bent on suffocating them
Shredding each declaration with false accounts
Blaming them for not being or being too much
Dismantle all hope with shame
Me Too is building a movement
Changing conversation
Shifting social consciousness
Freeing victims from the silent chains
It's because of an outspoken few
that others reclaim their power
Scribed our name in the cement next to theirs

Shelby "Mahogany" Wilson

Speak their stories loud and clear
Still with fear coupled with embarrassment
They stand in the light
Shouting in perfect pitch
Me Too

Denied Privileges

Remove the boxes
The ones marked with derogatory names
The fabricated labels
Attempting to keep me a prisoner
in a "free society."
Stripping me of privilege
Because WHAT I am not WHO I am
Eliminate the close-minded
Those who can't see
Pass impregnated thoughts of hatred
Choosing to err on the side of bigotry
Remove the titles that enforce a false hierarchy
Dressing up equality as "trendy."
Characterizing me as a threat to morality
Failing to rise when confronted
Standing along the sidelines
witnessing the injustice

Judgment and ridicule within the community
keeps the poison flowing easily
It's hard to find pride

Denied Privileges

When you are disowned by family
Cast aside like yesterday's trash
Broken from the inside
Made to believe your value is less
Conflicted by society's inconsistency
It shouldn't be a choice, but a God-given right
It's hard to forge ahead
When the majority would rather disassociate
Keep silent to maintain civility
I'd rather have all my civil liberties
Then be rated
A secondhand citizen in the land of the free

I'm not asking
I'm demanding
The poor depiction of who I am be removed
The defaming my character be retracted
I want the world to see me
Reverse the misrepresentation
Stand at the courthouse steps
Knowing I'm included in policy
I want the same rights without judgment
To stand hand in hand without shame
Walk without fear of retaliation
Respected
No apology for who I am
Loved
No guilt for being open
Honor
I will fight for my rights
Unite this community through words
Celebrate the oneness of all
Because I am the face of equity

Splintered

Public perceptions have splintered our community
Causing division within our culture
Sowing seeds of mistrust
Shattering unity
The fabric of our community fades with time
Each new generation outlines a new pattern
Delicate pins keep history in place
Outside forces confuse sexuality with identity
We are multicolored reams in random sequences
Complex textures of emotions
Spooling strands of diversity
in an already crowded community
Threading the needle
between acceptance and rejection
Slivers of light in a kaleidoscope of woven patches
Stigma of our being
Slowly unraveling the material along the edges
Causing a widening between the stitches
Tattering and fraying
Tussling with dissenting opinions

Splintered

Disintegrating the spectrum
Fading our vibrant colors
Reducing our visibility a quarter inch at a time
Scattering needles
Shards of glass in a fragile community

Multiple Stops

Before the first shot
It could have all been prevented
A single intervention
The moment he made the decision

Stop
The moment he devised a plan

Stop
The moment he obtained the guns

Stop
The moment he got in the car

Stop
The moment he pulled into the parking lot

Stop
The moment he stepped into the school yard

Stop

Multiple Stops

The moment before the first shot

Stop
He made a choice, and innocent lives were lost
Leaving family and friends with empty holes
May the Lord guide these lost souls

Pro Lives

I understand the argument
Pro Second Amendment
Gun rights for everyone except people of color
We are shot and killed for possession
Damn if we are legally permitted
"Don't take my guns."
is heard over my right to life

What about my right
to walk down a street without fear
In a country that continues to invalidate my being
Making brown people a statistic
Ignoring my right to breathe easily
On guard because of trigger-happy proud people
Yes, I'm offended

We are not seen as human beings
Equality doesn't include me
We are revered as the problem
Something to be punished or destroyed
Prison or grave

Pro Lives

My brothers and sisters are sacrificed daily
Not for crimes but being the wrong kind

Murdering us in vain
Defaming our names
Shedding blood to keep precious guns safe
Making us out to be the perpetrator
instead of the victim
Failing to recognize my life isn't bulletproof

People over guns
But not if you are pro Second Amendment
That's all it takes
Until things change
My rights will continue
To be reduced to a bumper sticker
A slogan that resonates with no significance

Guns matter not lives
Don't tell me to breathe
I'm suffocating under the bureaucracy
Better yet, who's breathing for the deceased

Gun Silence

They said no more, never again
As history repeats once again
Congress refuses to step in
Standing behind the 2nd Amendment
Blaming the mentally ill doesn't resolve the issue
Take some damn responsibility
AR-15's and assaults rifle riddle our communities
Creating warzones in our churches and schools
We ask when it will be enough
When is it time to act
When do we respond to hurt
The damage of gun violence
Mass shooting after mass shooting
Still no new legislation
Session after session
Crippled by the gun manufacturers and the NRA
Using social media
Defrauding and defaming all those who speak
Citing conspiracy
Sending prayers with no action
Lip service as people bury

Gun Silence

Their children, fathers, mothers or whole families
Instead of pep rallies, proms and graduations
We are attending funerals on the daily
Placing small bodies in caskets
Left with pictures and fragmented memories
How many tears must we cry
How many more must die
They would rather turn schools into prisons
Arming teachers with guns
Practice active shooter drills instead of protecting
Militarizing and desensitizing our children
These are the pills they force us to swallow
No solution to a growing problem
Congressional agendas and bipartisan allegiance
Too concerned about their legislative seat
Afraid of a backlash instead of safety
Worried about personal priorities
Over their communities
Bureaucracy and red tape
Blocked, rejected, and stalled protections
We refuse to play dead
while our government pretends to care
Silently hoping
We will give up the cause
They dropped the ball
We still have no law
They failed us all

Rolling Back History

Black Reality

Living in a bubble
Seduced by the power of society
Still believing in the good that men do
Reality is evil lives too
The dark thoughts plague the world
Tearing down dreams
Poisoning the streams
Killing the youth
Voices of the future
The world colors my view
Never understanding the corruption from the pew
Faith in God will protect us all
It didn't protect Sandra Bland or Freddie Gray
Fear of the law is a daily thought
Worrying about who's next on the list
My ignorance allows me to carry on blindly
Countless names chiming in my ears
Unknown faces float past my screen
Victimized and beaten repeatedly
I can't unhear their screams

Shelby "Mahogany" Wilson

My heart is beating with tears
What if the commander-in-chief were shot
I know our hearts will stop
Reminding us
Nothing is sacred

Rolling Back History

I thought I lived in America
Where the media was independent
Speaking out was a privilege
Holding government accountable was expected
Justice was blind

The flag was sacred
We fought for freedom
Believe in the words on the Statue of Liberty
Everyone has a place no matter the race
Women had entitlements
Religious freedoms were accepted

This country was built on so many ambitions
Modified decade after decade
Somehow a few changed the trajectory
A 900-page document rewrote history
Now we are living with a single objective
Turn back the clock in America
Reverse all the gains
Where the color of your skin reigns supreme

Rolling Back History

Male was the preferred gender
The perfect women were submissive

Somewhere we lost our vision
Rolling back independence
Censorship plagues the media
Dissenting voices are disappearing
As social media posts are blocked
Removed for exposing the truth

It didn't happen overnight
They have been slowly indoctrinating
Desensitizing through programming
I don't mean brainwashing or sorcery
I mean controlling the narrative
Posting propaganda
The nation was built on the premises we before me
Now people act like we are on TV
Human inadequacy has birthed greed
Sacrificing everyone for currency
Turning people into soulless corpses
Intimidating those who disagree
Promising violence instead of compromising

The voices are getting louder
Fertilizing the nation with seeds of hatred
Amending the American narrative
Eliminating portions while whitewashing the story
Exposing America's true history
The one that celebrated the birth of a nation
Founded the slave plantation

Welcome to America

There was no welcome to America
We were stripped of our crowns
Profile and defiled upon arrival
Beaten into submission
Never treated like a citizen
Constant struggle to be seen as human beings
It's a daily fight for my freedom and my rights

I was written as 3/5ths human
Property in the Constitution
Some still see me that way
Subjected to black pathology
Combating the rage of oppression
Wrath of aggression
Overcompensation due to suspicion
Constantly on alert

The game changed
From direct to institutional discrimination
Dismantling traditions
Systematically annihilating the family core nucleus

Welcome to America

Removing positive images
Methodically eliminating community resources
Creating a dismissive generation
Slowly reverting to open discrimination
Living while black is a statistical fact
The odds have increased

Welcome to America

Their discontent has been validated and revitalized
We are paying the price
They used to separate the good from
troublemakers
Now it's a stereotype BLACK
Subjecting everyone to the broken window policy
The racism is built in
Crafted to make us all criminals at first sight
Forget innocent until proven guilty
Ignore reasonable doubt
The color of my skin is my sin

How can I win a battle
When they poison the water
Defund neighbor programs
Eradicate the family community
Eliminate higher education opportunities
Discard the primary school
Generating an illiterate race
Mentally castrate the men
Diminish the mortality rate
Roll back protections through regulations
Victimize the children
Leaving the next generation defenseless

The system is rigged
But we weren't given an even playing field
They cloak it in reasonable accommodations
Instead of paying reparations
It's been 400 years since Fort Comfort
Welcome to America is a myth
Ideological wish
The lighter your skin
The better your reality

Welcome to America

For the rest of us
Its words inscribed on a statue
Symbol of hypocrisy
America's legacy

Slaves to Immigrants

Looking, searching for so-called illegals

Masked men roam our streets

Reminiscent of the men in white sheets
hunting people like me

Imprisoning those who walk without papers

Enslaving those who can't prove their freedom

Sending them to unnamed detention centers

Apprehending and imprisoning the innocent

Leaving families without recourse

Instilling fear in those who dream of escaping

Told the constitution doesn't apply

Slaves to Immigrants

You are property until you die

No rights extended until you pledge your allegiance

Demanding loyalty to a master and his family

Temporary acceptance
Unless you break the 13th Amendment

Chattel under the law

They arrived with the promise of a better life

Taken only to endure a life of strife

Removed because of racial profiling
Under a flawed presidency

Conquered and turned into property

Eradicate the illegals and restore slavery

Black skin farming the land

Make America great again

No rights or civil liberties

No claim to this land

An asset on a registry

Undocumented and criminalized

Slaves to Immigrants

Disregarding history

Forced to leave without a trace

Do you see

Its trickery taken place

A sleight of hand

We're pawns on a chessboard

Creating friction between races

A term created to keep us in place

Better to be divided than unified

Collusion disrupts power
Aids the disadvantaged

Pretending to be blind because of greed

They will succeed

The immigrants are not the enemy

We have become a victim of our tragedy

Struggling to feed their families
Establish legacy

They are a casualty of the unjust society

Slaves to Immigrants

Those masked men who roam the streets
 Looking for illegals

But when do they start looking for me?

ICE Police

Lawless thugs searching and hunting
Cruising the neighborhood in unmarked vehicles
Pretending to be enforcers
Shielding their faces from our community
Given blind immunity
Constantly abusing their authority
Vandalizing without repercussions

Color of your skin
Pretext for stopping and questioning
Detaining citizens to fulfill some mandate
Just another excuse to require papers
Using intimidation to prove their masculinity
Remembering justice is on their side
Endless resentment

Never failing to remind us of our position
Our freedom is a privilege
Badge and guns boosting confidence
Perceived threatening situation
Justification for escalation

ICE Police

We have been forced to relinquish our protection

Surrender our freedoms
All under the guise of security
Exposing the so-called illegals
Penalizing those seeking asylum
Not realizing our interference created the problem
People are becoming desensitized

Forgetting that they are brutalizing human beings
Ripping apart families
Devastating our economy
For what
For whom
Just so we can say we caught the illegals
One man's campaign promise
Based on a fabricated lie
Motivated a criminal enterprise
Wreaking havoc on Americans
Destroying evidence

Penalizing the press
Producing false narratives
Muddying the perception
Allowing deputized gangs to disrupt our country
Escaping under federal protection
Using our tax dollars to fund our oppression

Fear and anger don't encapsulate the frustration
We are being held hostage under false pretenses
Every day it becomes more intense
As citizens are being carted away
Justifying blind allegiance
To a man with a personal grievance

Basic Freedoms

We Live

We live in a society
Where it's ok to be nude on TV
But a child's hairstyle is under scrutiny
Come as you are to church
Not if you are dressed for a night in the club
Where killing a child
Accepted if you have a good case

Where freedom of speech
Permitted if you agree with me
Where people go missing in a city
Nobody finds it disturbing
We've come a long way
From working ourselves to death for a better life
It's ok to be proud of Section 8 if you represent

People would rather tear you down
Before they build you up
Where communication is texting
DM's, and X posting

Shelby "Mahogany" Wilson

We get our news from the internet
Newspapers are used for packing
You can be famous for doing nothing
Paid millions for frivolous lawsuits

Where reality TV is more popular than fantasy
Where libraries become tombs for books
because they're available on the Nook
We live in a society
That stops helping each other
Instead, it climbs over one another
We don't stab you in the back
We cut your throat and make a video

Our society has been deteriorating for years
As the generations become savvy
The core values become obsolete
People stop connecting and being present
Communities stop raising each other
Leaving our kids without role models

We live
We are a society
Our morals have not progressed with technology
Our social skills have fallen below the norm
We wonder why we are raising a nation of killers
Ill-equipped parents
The middle class has been diminished
We would rather be entertained than educated
Let TV and society raise our children

Stop complaining
We are still maintaining the status quo
Praying on Sunday

Progressive Lines Etched in Time's Brittle Glass

Gossiping during the week
We must change our perspective
Connect, empower, and support one another
Because like cancer it spreads when untreated
This society has been diagnosed with stage 4

Karenesity

Karens deceive people for a living
Misleading conversations
Creating phony accusations
Beware of false allegations
They are pros at fabrication
Venomous snakes striking without provocation
No shame in their vindictive game

Pretending to be a friend
Backstabbing enemy
Smiling in your face bringing office treats
They are agents of deceit
Cross them and you will see
They are a dangerous breed
Toxic to all they meet

Gossiping with cruel intentions
Giving false testimony to enhance their position
They are mean-spirited
Leaving land mines for the unsuspecting
Undermining others to seem important

Karenesity

Inserting themselves into other people's business
Pretending to be of assistance

Beware of the entitled ones
Master manipulators
Always acting like the world owes them
They are the first to call a manager
Pretending to be victimized to obtain sympathy
Turning on the fake tears to gain attention
But don't be fooled is a trademark position

They have a hidden agenda
Poisoning the well with misinformation
Envy and jealousy are the root of treachery
Secretly scheming
Calculating behind the scenes
It is a damn shame when talent is wasted
And the Oscar goes to Karen in the workplace

Living While Black

It's not safe to be Black in America
Driving while Black
has always been a problem
We now must be cautious while
picking up trash
Leering in a coffee shop
Warrants unwanted detention
Questioned about our gym
membership
Walking in your neighborhood is
suspicious

Vacationing at a bed and breakfast
is considered mischievous
Don't complain about your server
cause that's an arresting offense
Who knew that hanging in the
backyard could be so dangerous
It's become a liability
to be out after the streetlights

Living While Black

Even using the bathroom
on planes
has become an inconvenience
Golfing respectfully can elicit a
complaint

We must never break rules or color
outside the lines
That's an automatic fine
We are profiled
from the moment we enter a room
Dissected and rejected
before given
opportunity
Made to feel like we are a threat
Our very presence is the pretense

Portrayed as a predator
But what about our protection
Ensuring our safety
from the trigger-happy
law enforcement
The biased storekeepers
The nosey neighbors
It's built-in discrimination
We are criminalized
and dehumanized
based on predetermined
conclusions

It was never safe to be
Black in America
From slavery to lynching
to daily executions

Living While Black

Nothing has changed
We are still seen as a danger
A wild animal
that needs to be tamed
Which causes our underlying pain

The frustrations and anger
are contained
But how much longer
must we endure
before we are seen as human
We have been silently marching
Protesting racism
Praying on Sunday
But the system is designed
to keep us cornered

Video and live feed
only reveal the daily struggle
Subjected to regular abuse
based on color
We call it prejudice
But the truth lies within
Perception has been colored
Allowing those fears to separate
Divided into two categories
Them and us

Bonded by the internal factors
Intern creating a hostel reality
We have been told we are free
Yet we are constantly battling
social injustice and inequality
Where is civility

Living While Black

or common decency
Never applied to people of color
A reminder, it was never safe
To be Black in America

Freedom's Price Tag

The color of freedom
has always come at an expense
Taxed for voting
Taxed for my skin
Taxed for being a woman
Instead of collecting dividends
I'm collecting fees
Receiving dimes and pennies
for recycled words of hope

Limited by social constraints
and unspoken contracts
The return on investment for living
While Black exceeds my life expectancy
There are no legacy discounts or sales
It's full price
We are living in a space
where twice as good is the fee, you pay
When your skin is darker than the copier paper

Freedom's Price Tag

Pristine resumes with accomplishments
are not stamps of approval
Step out of line and you will be fined
Microaggression embedded in coded language
Constantly observing every word and action
Instead of progressing we are digressing
160 years of provisional freedom
Filled Jim Crow and separate but equal
My independence just turned 51

Baby boomers are the last generation of segregation
Controlling the halls of justice
Assessing fees for basic privileges
Criminalizing skin and demonizing existence
Our freedom is more fragile than you think
It all comes down to a stroke of a pen
Nine court justices, nine votes
Removing Rights and freedoms
based on party lines

Delegitimizing civil rights
won on merit versus privilege
Praising the holy amendments
The ones that preach freedom of speech
Right to bear arms
The 15th and 19th gave me the right to have a say
Every 25 years it can be taken away

We have been paying with black lives
Churches are erecting phony gods
Making martyrs out of deceivers
Drowning out the voices of truth speakers
How quickly we forget the stories and pictures
Enslaved ancestors vanish

Freedom's Price Tag

from books and museums
Our contributions are being
Repackaged and colonized

DEI (Diversity, Equity, and Inclusion)
Affirmation action is the new leprosy
Deduction from your federal income
If your programs include everyone
The gap for financial freedom is widening
Opportunity for advancement
vanishes like stars in the night

We were given 60 years.
60 years to gather wealth
build a strong community
To make an impact
Where we were told
Our words have the potential to unleash freedom
To empower the people
To invoke a moment
To shift a nation

Everyone has a voice, even the dead
But the current administration
is penalizing those who speak
They value censorship and supremacy
over the right to have autonomy
Our voices are being silenced
for speaking against hypocrisy

I recognize this may be the last day to speak freely
Last time before a fine is imposed on my creativity
Last time before I am outed for speaking boldly
Vocalizing my outrage

Freedom's Price Tag

Last time before my words are levied
Assessed with monetary value
The last time
before my words are stripped of meaning
I'm charged or imprisoned
for having the audacity to speak freely

Untapped Wealth

We walk this land with hopes and dreams
Visioning a better future for the youth
Enriched with generational wealth
Blessed with health
We speak in caution
Allowing our ancestors to guide us
Leaving a trail of untold stories
Unspoken truths

We are listening
Awakening to the ancestral voices
Lifting our minds through the clearing
Envisioning more than Rosewood
Establishing thriving communities
Like Jackson Ward or the Greenwood District
We are empowering minds
Influencing intellect by passing knowledge
Patenting our intellectual property
Guarding our original creations

Building an encrypted cyber network

Untapped Wealth

Hidden investors
Teaching the value of appreciation
wealthy vs depreciation
Money earned
Isn't always spent rather it's invested
Compound interest with dividends
Continuous cash flow is obtainable
We possess skills and untouched capital
Underutilized endless possibilities

We are divided by outside sources
Afraid of our true value and potential
Commodities sold to the highest bidder
Never invested in the black community
Watching our wealth be depleted
Failing to plant our money tree

Voting Voice

Broken System

The courts are being perverted
They are appointing
untested lawyers in the seat of power
Diluting the system with biased judges
Preventing us from receiving a fair decision
They are making exceptions to the law
Replacing prior judicial precedent
Allowing corruption to supersede the constitution
Using the justice system to silence the opposition
Dismantling the three levels of government
Rendering them devoid of agency
Unable to reverse policy
Dismantling democracy
Demolishing the legal remedy
Leaving us without any real possibilities
Unable to obtain justice
Calling attention to poor decisions
The harm being inflicted
Turning our pain into a frivolous case
The words still ring, "No Justice, No Peace."
They cut deeper knowing they have no validity

Shelby "Mahogany" Wilson

The privilege to criticize is being rescinded
Our voices are being protested
Removing every achievement
It's not being televised or heard over the airways
They are chipping away with strategic cases
Using the underlying grievance to overturn a decree
There are no objections
They render our voice useless
Permitting police brutality without penalty
Violating a woman's right to privacy
Granting men unlimited autonomy
Removing guardrails
Leaving no one to protect the defenseless
Those deemed vulnerable in the eyes of society
The system has always been inconsistent
Filled with regulations to prevent resistance
Giving preferential treatment to those of means
Leaving the rest to pay the price
With every new judgement
The noose becomes tighter
Choking out the sounds of the unprotected
Imprisoning our voices
until only death hears our screams

Morning After

Somber faces and empty halls
Roads deserted like the hope of this country
I mourn her already
The loss is great
Grief spreads through the fabric of a nation
We awaken to a white male-dominated society
Staring at my own ceiling
Pondering how high I will rise
In a country destined to remove women's rights
Strip civil liberties by chipping at the foundation
Shattering the bridge
I was not disillusioned
I allowed myself to be swept up
Hoping for a different outcome
Belief we would finally have a voice
It was time for a new reign to lead
I imagined this country
Embracing her like a true leader
Accepting her with open arms
Fully accepted by the masses
The dream of a woman at the helm

Morning After

We failed
They turn out
Smashed hope like fragile glass
Slapped America's hand
Left an imprint upon my soul
like scars from a hot iron
So many promises were built on phony pledges
Failed American experiment
Denied membership to the secret club
They pulled the rug
Revealing the truth
We will never possess enough power
to overtake the private society
that governs from its perch of supremacy
Secretly forging documents
Ensuring our voices remain silent
Limiting the flow of money
Guaranteeing subordinance
To maintain the hierarchy
They never believed she was the one
We mourn the idea
The dream
The fantasy

Judas In Disguise

He said he would turn
our American streets into training grounds
Bringing military force
Enforcing his need for allegiance
Converging on sanctuary cities
ICE is America's version of Germany's Gestapo
Weaponizing law enforcement
Indoctrinating the citizens through propaganda
Gradually implementing fascist policies
Trading safety for government protection
Watching as they push the boundaries of liberty
Endorsing political persecution
Sanctioning partisan corruption
Slowly normalizing violence against people of color
Not realizing we are being herded like lambs
Pitting us against one another to advance their plans
Hypnotizing the masses through paid media
Memorializing a man
constantly vocalized white supremacy
Exploiting human weakness
Defunding anyone who dares speak independently

Judas In Disguise

Systematically dismantling communities
Those bloated promises are conditional
Blinded by false loyalty
Placing our faith in the misguided leaders
Everyone is disposable
Sacrificing human life for the almighty dollar
Even Jesus was deceived by Judas

Eliminating Power

Pull the alarms
Sound the sirens
We are under attack
Our voting rights are being snatched
This administration
Is gutting our ability to participate
Cutting us out of the process
Eliminating our voices
Diminishing our influence
Stripping our independence
Removing our representation
One vote
One person
The Supreme Court
Delivering a devastating decision
Underestimate the implications
There will be consequences
Independent voting is being extinguished
They are sealing our fate
Checkmate
We will no longer be considered

Eliminating Power

Our voices will be dismissed
Shrinking under the elected
Sworn to protect it
Greed and power are the chosen leaders
We used to govern with civility
Now it is about who controls money
Focusing on race and religion
A distraction against the real enemy
Abolishing impartial voting
They are deconstructing the 15th amendment
Neutralizing its significant
Arguing that color doesn't matter
92 years of Jim Crow
taught us the importance of having an opportunity
Over time it's been minimized
Believing our votes were irrelevant
Only to be eliminated
We needed those voices
Not to speak but in voting
To keep those from stealing our elections
Violating our civil rights
Nullifying our protections under the law
Shattering our right to safety
Denying protection for privacy
The right to vote establishes boundaries
Instills liberty
All it took was one power hungry congress
To topple an entire nation

Disgraced Legacy

Temporary tenants are debasing the Oval Residence
Designing a gilded palace
Nothing represents the standards of the People's
    House
Turning the Presidency into a celebrity gameshow
Auctioning the nation's business like a commercial
Strategically airing propaganda videos

Technology is changing our perception
Deep fakes modifying social media
Weaponizing AI to manipulate and humiliate
Placing targets on American citizens
Sending a dangerous message
This is not our government

Ignoring the presidential oath
To protect and defend the Constitution
Neglecting the nation's pleas
While flaunting his greed
Pardoning charlatans
Celebrating the Christian nationalism

Disgraced Legacy

Revealing the country's division
Neglecting his duties to pursue his own mission

Creating chaos through confusion
Lying without hesitation
Continuing to divide the nation
Playing games with its reputation
No longer a destination

Detaining legal residents
To satisfy a bogus quota
Turning everyone into the enemy of the state
Tanking the American economy
with tariffs and wealthy freebies
Disenfranchising the underprivileged
Regurgitating fabricated
Information to control the narrative

We elected a con artist with a record
A man without character
Running a scam through the presidency
He came with no strategy
Armed with false ideologies
America is under siege

They are creating a new legacy
Ignited by the 1619 Project
Fueled by Project 2025
Driven by white fragility and a toxic history
enabling the rise of a monarchy

Death of Democracy

Tyranny is encroaching on our democracy
America is slowly becoming an occupancy
Painful to see the decay of morality
Creeping along the underbelly of society
Watching humanity bleed on the concrete
Witnessing the fall of a country
Poised for greatness only to wither under hatred
Crumbling under the hypocrisy and greed
Revenge disguised as patriotism
Creating a new breed of corporatism
Camouflage as capitalism
Shielding Cronyism
No longer a beacon of freedom
Too late for redemption
Overrun by temptation
Left with a broken nation without salvation

Acknowledgments

I want to thank my family for always being supportive. You are the foundation of my world. I give special thanks to my partner and friend Eli Andrews. You are my heart and personal cheerleader in life. Thank you, Cia Thompson. Our conversations have been inspirational; they restarted a passion and set my pen on fire. I want to thank my brother, Reginald G Wilson, for the hours and dedication to helping me create a meaningful cover. I also want to thank all the friends and family who took the time to proofread my poetry. I also thank those who listened and craved more, providing me with the fuel to keep expressing myself through spoken and written words. The universe has assembled an incredible group of individuals to guide me on this journey. I am so grateful to every single person in my life.

About the Author

Shelby "Mahogany" Wilson has lived in Alaska for over 30 years. A published poet, Wilson began her journey with the Alaska Poetry League. In 2005, she was the fourth runner-up in the Alaska slam contest. Since then, she has expanded her creative resume to include performance poet, workshop facilitator, writer, spiritual counselor, motivational speaker, and

Pink Ice Gala for Cancer, Take Back the Night for STAR (Standing Together Against Rape). She has performed at the Celebration of Change presented by Radical Arts for Women. She has opened for other creatives like Triple Blak and Reggie Ward.

Her published works include *Serenity* (2006), *Broken Wings, Mending Damaged Souls* (2009), *In My Lifetime: Wonders* (2012); "She Did it Anyway" *Alaska Women Speak* (2012); *Verbal Stimulations* (2015); *BeautiFly* (2016), *Building Fires in the Snow, a Collection of Alaska LGBT Short Fiction and Poetry* (2016).

www.SoulofMahogany.com